planning for strategic communication

a workbook for applying social theory to professional practice

JOHN A. McARTHUR, Ph.D.

Copyright © 2014   John A. McArthur

All rights reserved.

Cover art and formatting by J.A. McArthur
www.jamcarthur.com

ISBN: 1497329396
ISBN-13: 978-1497329393

Table of Contents

Introduction	1
Planning Strategic Communication: A Flexible Template	7
Applying Berger: Narrative Analysis	15
Applying Bourdieu: Capital Analysis	21
Applying Foucault: Discourse Archaeology	27
Applying Giddens: Structural Analysis	35
Applying Goffman: Impression Analysis	41
Applying Habermas: Discourse Analysis	49
Applying Putnam: Social Analysis	57
Applying Weber: Legitimacy Claim Analysis	65
About the Author	71

Introduction

Here begins my quest to help strategic communicators add value and gravitas to the way they do business.

Over the past ten years, I've written, revised, reviewed, or consulted on countless strategic communication plans. The one concept that separates the exceptional plans from the mediocre attempts is a foundational framework for innovation.

Creating a strategic communication plan has long been more art than science. Those who were exceptional artists could weave intricate stories and concepts together for their clients. Others sought to replicate their artistry by mimicking and adapting good work and applying it to different business and communication settings. The goal of the information herein is to inspire a little more "science" in our field. Admittedly, this science is a loose one by many standards. But, the combination of the beautiful artistry and a firm foundation of theory can help practitioners build vibrant and innovative plans that move our communication goals forward.

I'm not alone in my quest. For too long, the merging fields of strategic communication have established themselves as fields of practice, with limited connection to theory, reflection, or introspection. This realization sparked a revolution of sorts (at least in academic circles). When the *International Journal of Strategic Communication* launched its first issue in 2009, the editors set out to define the field: strategic communication is "the purposeful use of communication by an organization to fulfill its mission." [1] They noted that the field overall might contain the vast work that falls into disparate but connected units of business practice: management, marketing, public relations, technical communication, political communication, and information and social marketing campaigns. And, all of these units engage in the process of developing and implementing plans for strategic communication.

The bottom line is this: clients and co-workers can tell the difference between a plan that is a well-presented hodge-podge of ideas and a plan that is deeply rooted in a conceptual framework. Noted futurist Howard Rheingold has labeled this 21st century skill as "crap detection." [2]

In the world of strategic communication, clients are becoming leery of the increasing number of entrepreneurs masquerading as consultants. Many search for consultants who can bring true knowledge and innovation to their work. Therefore, as consultants, our job is to become not only artists of beautiful plans, but scientists that root our plans in theory and endeavor to test the results. This process – gathering information, interpreting results, developing appropriate strategies from our analyses, and testing their merit – requires a foundation in some theoretical base.

I'm not advocating for all consultants to adopt a similar theoretical base. We've tried that before. The resilient SWOT analysis (strengths, weaknesses, opportunities, threats) persists as the leading framework for plans today. But, I question whether it is the best suited framework for the multiplicity of communication problems facing daily practice in the field.

I suggest quite the opposite. Engaging with a wide variety of theories can harness all sorts of different lenses and opportunities for innovation. As a field, the time has come for us to test and investigate theories in a way that

---

[1] Hallahan, K., Holtzhausen, D., van Ruler, B. Vercic, D., & Sriramesh, K. (2007). Defining Strategic Communication. *International Journal of Strategic Communication, 1* (1), p. 3.

[2] Rheingold, H. (2010). Attention and other 21st century literacies. Retrieved from http://www.educause.edu/ero/article/attention-and-other-21st-century-social-media-literacies

can move our study and our business practice forward. Theorists Øyvind Ihlen and Betteke van Ruler argue for this practice: "It can be seen as a sign of maturity for a discipline to contain different, comparative schools of thought and to rest on different theoretical foundations."[3] The theories presented herein have been applied to public relations and related fields by scholars and practitioners with varying degrees of difficulty and success.

Over the past five years, I have had the good fortune of working with numerous business people, marketers, entrepreneurs, executives, and employees invested in the study of communication for the betterment of their workplaces. We've tested the applicability of theory for a variety of contexts. My place in academia has also afforded me the opportunity to consult with theoreticians far more brilliant than myself on the nature of these theories and ways they might be translated for practice. The outcome of these experiences and consultations is this worktext. Herein, readers will find a diverse subset of frameworks for devising plans for strategic communication using theory as a foundation.

This work is largely based on my experience with the concepts presented in *Public Relations and Social Theory*,[4] a book which set out to test the mental and causal limits of theory in the practice of strategic communication. The edited collection of chapters is rich fodder for practice in our field and has inspired many students over the years to engage thoughtfully and thoroughly in the reflective work required in our field. It is a bit dense at times, but its impact can be firmly felt throughout the information here. In some ways, this workbook might actually emerge as a practical supplement to the vast theoretical knowledge in that excellent text.

Readers of *Public Relations and Social Theory* will note that some theories discussed are not included here. The selected theories here were chosen because they have demonstrated tangible applications in real-world settings in the process of planning for strategic communication.

---

[3] Ihlen, Ø., and van Ruler, B (2009). Applying Social Theory to Public Relations. In Ihlen, Ø., van Ruler, B., & Fredriksson, M. (2009). *Public Relations and Social Theory*. New York: Routledge, p. 4.

[4] Ihlen, Ø., van Ruler, B., & Fredriksson, M. (2009). *Public Relations and Social Theory*. New York: Routledge.

How to Use this Book

This book contains far less writing than this introduction might suggest. It is less a textbook and more a workbook. The sections that follow articulate a series of theories and their potential application for planning strategic communication.

In the first section, readers will find a template for planning strategic communication. This template, while highly flexible and largely situation-dependent, illustrates the major components that are generally pieces of a standard plan for strategic communication.

Subsequent sections address theories primed for application, one theory at a time. These theories come from a diversity of social perspectives over the last century. As in the *Public Relations and Social Theory* text, the theories are presented in alphabetical order by the theorists' last names.

For best results, a plan for strategic communication would want to select one of the theories and use that theory in its entirety to develop the plan.

This may be the most important note in the process of developing a plan. Use the whole theory. As foundations for a communication plan, these theories only add value if they are allowed to fully investigate the situation at hand.

Consultants who pick and choose one component of this theory and one component of that theory are simply continuing in our old practice of artistry – using myself to define my approach. Instead, the utilization of a theory in its entirety affords consultants a comprehensive foundation to articulate the good and bad (and the gray areas) in a situation. A comprehensive approach requires the consultant to engage multiple angles of a situation and inspires innovation unknown to the consultant at the start of the planning process. This is the role of science in an artistic field – to inspire innovation that adds to our conversation.

The theoretical sections are presented with an explanation and then a workbook style series of pages to help inspire the work of consultants using the theory. I encourage you to write in the appropriate areas in the workbook (and scribble across the other areas as well), use the margins, and jot down ideas. You may even find it beneficial to take the same situation and try out three or four theories in your analysis to see what theory makes the most sense to apply.

Critics of this approach will argue that this process overly simplifies the theories into a toolbox for consultants. Those critics would be correct. This workbook is an attempt to apply theory to practice in some tangible ways that can drive forward our thinking in strategic communication practice. As you work with these theories, if you find a strategy that really resonates, contact me so that we can contribute a case study or article back to the academic discussion of theory in practice.

The strange thing about these theories, in my experience, is that some theories are better suited to some situations than others. Consultants will find that particular situations lend themselves to specific theories. When using this workbook, if a theory doesn't make sense for the situation at hand, move on to a different one. Not every theory will apply to every situation.

The ultimate goal of this worktext is to help identify theoretical approaches that reap benefits for communication practice. Then, using the guidelines in the text, to develop plans for strategic communication practice that have impact.

I encourage you to use this text well and contact me if you have ideas that diverge from mine. And, if you find yourself in need of an outside consultant, which we all do from time to time, feel free to give me a call.

John A. McArthur, Ph.D

Planning Strategic Communication: A Flexible Template

Planning for strategic communication practice can take many forms. What follows in this section is a template for creating a formal plan for strategic communication. Plan creators take a fair amount of artistic license in crafting plans, so this template lists the major sections that will likely exist in most plans.

A plan for strategic communication should be narrowly focused on one particular situation, event, or problem. A narrow focus allows the consultant to dig deeply into the organization and use theory to hone specific communicative practices present in the situation.

Consultants will also want to be sure to investigate the mission, vision, and values of the organization. Remember that strategic communication has been defined as "the purposeful use of communication by an organization to fulfill its mission." [5] Without a knowledge of the mission, a consultant cannot

---

[5] Hallahan, K., Holtzhausen, D., van Ruler, B. Vercic, D., & Sriramesh, K. (2007). Defining Strategic Communication. *International Journal of Strategic Communication, 1* (1), p. 3.

> **Major Components of a
> Typical Plan for Strategic Communication**
>
> I. Executive Summary
>
> II. Purpose
>
> III. Rationale
>
> IV. Analysis
>
> V. Market Impacts
>
> VI. Suggested Strategies
>
> VII. Conclusion
>
> VIII. Appendices, including references

make any justifiable claims about an organization's strategy. The organization's mission should be one of the primary drivers of the plan.

A typical plan for strategic communication has 8 sections: executive summary, purpose, rationale, analysis, market impacts, strategies, conclusion, and appendices. Some plans have other sections (e.g. financial impacts, timelines, resource needs, etc.), depending on the specific needs of the organization and the situation addressed. The plan's author has significant control over the needs of the plan and the sections included. Thus, this section is meant to be a guide for successful plans. The material is adapted specifically for plans for strategic communication from the work presented in *Engage!* [6] and other strategic planning texts.

---

[6] Solis, B. (2010). Engage! The complete guide for brands and businesses to build, cultivate, and measure success in the new web. Hoboken, NJ: John Wiley & Sons, Inc.

Executive Summary

The executive summary is a synopsis of the entire document. It should provide a "tight, high-level summary of intentions, tactics, and metrics."[7] A quick read of the executive summary should give a full overview of what the reader would find if (s)he read the plan. Many consultants insert page references into the executive summary so that a read of the narrative summary also provides a table of contents for the plan. The executive summary is often formatted as one full, well-designed page.

Purpose

The purpose section should state the specific, narrow purpose of this plan. This should be the shortest portion of the plan and could be encapsulated in one or two well-crafted sentences.

Rationale

The rationale section addresses the challenge and opportunity present in the situation that necessitates a plan for strategic communication. It might articulate the particular type of strategic communication, or a particular product, service, or a new tactic the organization wants to employ. Most plans would list the organization's mission, vision, and values in this section. Additionally, this section typically advocates for the connection between the organization's mission and the need for the plan. The rationale section might be comprised of multiple paragraphs or pages of information, depending on the complexity of the situation at hand.

Analysis

In the analysis section, the consultant should utilize one of the theoretical frameworks herein to assess *the current state of the organization*. Whereas a plan might have formerly employed a SWOT analysis, the theoretical analyses in this document offer a broader variety of applicable models that innovate beyond a SWOT

---

[7] Solis, B. (2010). Engage! The complete guide for brands and businesses to build, cultivate, and measure success in the new web. Hoboken, NJ: John Wiley & Sons, Inc., p. 277.

approach. Study each subsequent chapter for guidance about how to apply each theory. The length of the analysis section is dependent on the scope of the analysis, but this section represents the bulk of the plan.

Market Impacts

The market impacts section may serve one of three different purposes, depending on the nature of the plan:
1. The section might describe types of communication that would reach each target public necessary for the strategic communication plan. If this is the case, the consultant would break down the audience into specific publics. For each public:
    - describe the public
    - explain specific challenges for reaching this public
    - explain the values of this public
    - describe the means (media) used to currently reach this public
    - explain how the public makes decisions
    - explain the public's current perception and sentiment
2. The section might discuss and describe competing communication in the communication arena. If this is the case, the consultant might choose to assess the success of similar or contrasting communicative messages in the situation addressed.
3. The section might address communication networks, channels, and pathways necessary for addressing the communication issues at hand. If this is the case, this section might incorporate visual representations of communication flow in the organization.

The length of this section varies widely.

Suggested Strategies

The suggested strategies are the products of the plan. This is the point at which the consultant gives recommendations based upon the analysis section of the plan. Strategies should address *the future state of the organization*. Strategies should be clearly organized around the theoretical framework selected (see how this works for each

framework later in this workbook). For each strategy suggested, the consultant should address any or all of the following as applicable:
- give a recommendation
- describe the strategy
- explain how the strategy supports the mission of the organization
- offer a timeline for implementation
- note any required resources including budget, supplies, expertise, and personnel (if needed) and their responsibilities
- suggest metrics and identify achievable goals

The length of this section is dependent on the number of strategies presented. If strategies become numerous, be sure to also include a concluding section that orders strategies by priority.

Conclusion

In the conclusion, the plan should offer further "realistic and creative ideas that get decision makers thinking about the possibilities and potential"[8] of successful strategic communication. A savvy consultant would use this section to provide ideas about next steps, and offer recommendations to the organization that include opportunities for the consultant to engage in future collaborative work. This section should include a few paragraphs at the most.

Appendices

The number and type of appendices included in a plan are totally dependent on the type of communication studied and the needs of the organization. Consultants might include references or endnotes as appendices, in addition to any documentation that informs the plan.

Again, the nature of the communication plan is that it can be adapted to the needs of the particular organization and situation. Sections might be

---

[8] Solis, B. (2010). Engage! The complete guide for brands and businesses to build, cultivate, and measure success in the new web. Hoboken, NJ: John Wiley & Sons, Inc., p. 280.

reordered, compressed, expanded, or revised to successfully target the issues at hand.

Formatting the Plan for Strategic Communication

One of the most common questions that persists surrounding the development of a plan is format. Plans take on different formats for different audiences and modes of presentation. Consultants may have to draft written plans and also present them orally and visually. Usually, the planning process results in at least a written plan, from which other media can be developed.

Before formatting a plan, authors should be sure that the writing in the plan is clear and concise. The plan should be free from errors in spelling and grammar. In addition, the sentence structures should allow for quick reading.

The following guidelines are suggestions for format that can help the written plan become highly readable so that content can be the focus. Readability is a natural goal for a written document. The field of technical communication (also part of strategic communication) has advanced our knowledge of how people read documents. In *Design that Delivers: Formatting Information for Print and Online Documents,*[9] authors Martha Andrews Nord and Beth Tanner offer that document designers should consider ease of reading, accessibility, comprehension, retention, and aesthetics when designing print documents.

In their definition, ease of reading is comprised of the layout, typeface and size of letters, spacing (between letters and between lines), and contrast between letters and page. Formatting for a plan might then include single (1.00-1.15) line spacing with line breaks as needed; a well-chosen typeface and size; and use of white space on the page for impact. This concept explains why the executive summary might best be fit onto one cover page while the

---

[9] Nord, M.A., & Tanner, B. (1992). Design that Delivers – Formatting Information for Print and Online Documents. In Barnum, C. & Carliner, S. *Techniques for Technical Communicators.* London: Longman, p. 221-225.

next page would start with the purpose. The plan would then flow across pages throughout the other sections.

Accessibility, in their guide, refers to the reader's ability to scan the document for visual cues demonstrating importance. This might include headers, bullets, menus, a table of contents, figures with captions, or other visual symbols for navigation. Often for a plan, headers help dramatically. Headers, indentations, and line breaks can be used together to create a list-like effect among the strategies, for example, that demonstrates visually the natural division between ideas.

For Nord and Tanner, comprehension refers to the reader's ability to understand the document. This is an issue of clarity, but it is also an issue of design. Comprehension is tied to audience. When formatting the document, consider how the audience might best be able to understand the information presented. In the plan, citations come into play here. Citation styles like APA and MLA function well to direct readers to external sources, but they detract from readability. Many plan authors have found success using footnotes or endnotes to drive readers to external sources without damaging the document's flow.

Retention, in their model, refers to the document's ability to remind the reader not only what is in the document but where it is in the document. In this case, the executive summary can really aid this process if it also functions as a kind of table of contents with page number references. Page numbers, section headers, and intentionally repeated design features can also increase retention.

Finally, Nord and Tanner point to aesthetics in document design. The reader has to want to read the document. The physical attractiveness is a key component of the document's overall design. Whether submitted in print or digital format, the written plan has the opportunity to look professional and well-constructed.

John A. McArthur

Applying Berger: Narrative Analysis

A narrative analysis applies Berger's social constructionist approach[10] to strategic communication. Such analysis examines a perceived reality and looks behind the initial reality to perceive how messaging produces a dominant narrative in the mind of audience. A narrative analysis might work well for a strategic communication plan that was working through an entrenched company identity or entrenched community understanding of a situation.

In the analysis phase, the assessor engages in a process of discovery by asking constituents various questions that allow the assessor to define and/or discover the major dominant narratives or messages contributing to the communication issue at hand. This list of dominant messages should be presented in the analysis with detailed descriptions of each narrative and its historical and current roots.

---

[10] For further information on Berger's theory and its application for strategic communication, see Heide, M. (2009). *On Berger.* In Ihlen, Ø., van Ruler, B., & Fredriksson, M. (2009). *Public Relations and Social Theory.* New York: Routledge.

Then, in the strategy phase, the assessor evaluates each dominant message or claim using one or multiple motifs:
- Debunking motif
- Unrespectability motif
- Relativization motif
- Cosmopolitan motif

The goal of an plan using these motifs would be the creation of a new or revised group reality. The motifs should help to answer the question, how can we debunk (for example) this perceived reality in our situation.

Worksheet for a Narrative Analysis

Jot down, based on observations and interviews, any narratives that contribute to the communication problem at hand.
These might include assumptions repeatedly voiced by members of the organization, narratives about historical practices, stories about why things are done a certain way, or similar shared identities.

Narrative Analysis

Identify major themes in your notes and list them here. These are likely the dominant narratives in the situation.

Choose one theme from above and describe the historical and current situations that led to the presence of this narrative in the organization. In your analysis section, repeat this process for each major theme you identified.

Working with the theme identified above, determine which motif (debunking, unrespectability, relativization, or cosmopolitan) could be suited to refute the narrative. Describe a process for refuting the narrative. In your strategy section, repeat this process for each theme identified. (Note that an organization might want to refute a "this is how we've always done it" narrative but reinforce a "we value our employees" narrative. If a theme needs reinforcement, say so).

A brief guide to the four motifs[11]:
- Debunking: seeing through the initial mask of a narrative to address its underlying goals.
- Unrespectability: considering the work of other people outside of one's own situation or position in the organization.
- Relativization: appreciating and incorporating the values of diverse audiences within the communication situation.
- Cosmopolitan: openness to yet-untested ideas and attitudes.

---

[11] See Heide, M. (2009). *On Berger*. In Ihlen, Ø., van Ruler, B., & Fredriksson, M. (2009). *Public Relations and Social Theory*. New York: Routledge, pp. 46-47.

Look back at the themes identified. What other questions do you need to ask the organization to tailor your suggestions to the organization's mission?

John A. McArthur

Applying Bourdieu: Capital Analysis

A capital analysis, based in Bourdieu's concepts surrounding field[12], suggests a broad survey of the symbolic and material resources available to an organization in a particular scenario. For situations related to resource needs and challenges, a capital analysis can reveal the variety of capital present and the areas of need for an organization, in hopes that directed, focused effort can build capital.

In the analysis phase, the assessor describes the resources present in a communication scenario in five categories:
- Institutionalization
- Economic capital
- Knowledge capital
- Social capital
- Symbolic capital

---

[12] For further information on Bourdieu's theory and its application for strategic communication, see Ihlen, Ø . (2009). *On Bourdieu*. In Ihlen, Ø., van Ruler, B., & Fredriksson, M. (2009). *Public Relations and Social Theory*. New York: Routledge.

In the strategy phase, the assessor uses the facts of the communication scenario presented to discern avenues for successful practice and uses the following framework for offering suggested strategies for the scenario:
- Strategies for utilizing institutionalization
- Strategies for developing economic capital
- Strategies for developing knowledge capital
- Strategies for developing social capital
- Strategies for developing symbolic capital

Worksheet for a Capital Analysis

As you investigate the organization, use this chart to make notes of the types of capital that contribute to the communication situation. These sections should lay the foundation for the structure of an analysis section. In the analysis take each form of capital separately and for each of the five sections:
(1) describe the components that contribute to capital in this area and,
(2) discuss how they are being currently applied.

A brief guide to the types of capital[13]:
- Institutionalization: structures that provide meaning in an organization (rules, policies, procedures, signs, etc.)
- Economic Capital: financial resources, real property, etc.
- Knowledge Capital: skills, education, expertise, etc.
- Social Capital: relational connections
- Symbolic Capital: organizational or individual prestige or notoriety

---

[13] See Ihlen, Ø. (2009). *On Bourdieu*. In Ihlen, Ø., van Ruler, B., & Fredriksson, M. (2009). *Public Relations and Social Theory*. New York: Routledge.

Capital Analysis

Current Patterns of Institutionalization

Current Economic Capital

Current Knowledge Capital

Current Social Capital

Current Symbolic Capital

Working from the notes you made above, describe opportunities the organization has to either:
(1) leverage the capital you noted, or
(2) expand its capital in an area of deficiency, or
(3) do both.

This will form the foundation for the strategies section of the plan. Discuss the suggestions for each form of capital separately in this section similar to the analysis. Whereas the analysis addressed the current state of capital in the organization, the strategies should discuss the future/possible roles of capital in the organization.

Capital Analysis

Strategies for developing Patterns of Institutionalization

Strategies for developing Economic Capital

Strategies for developing Knowledge Capital

Strategies for developing Social Capital

Strategies for developing Symbolic Capital

Applying Foucault:
Discourse Archaeology

A discourse archaeology, based in Foucault's practice of applying archaeology and genealogy to language[14], is a method for assessing the discourse occurring in a communicative situation. For scenarios related to an isolated communication message that creates power (realized or imagined) in an organization, a discourse archaeology approach can uncover the foundations of discourse and re-vision future communication.

In the analysis phase, the assessor first traces the discourse or communicative act in question back to its origins. Using an archaeological method, the discourse being examined uncovers the roots of the legitimacy of a communicative event.

Then, the assessor identifies discourse technologies active in the scenario:
- Technologies of production

---

[14] For further information on Foucault's theory and its application for strategic communication, see Motion, J., & Leitch, S. (2009). *On Foucault.* In Ihlen, Ø., van Ruler, B., & Fredriksson, M. (2009). *Public Relations and Social Theory.* New York: Routledge.

- Technologies of sign systems
- Technologies of power
- Technologies of self

In the strategy phase, the assessor addresses the means whereby the communicative act or scenario might be transformed or delegitimized using the technologies available or proposed:
- Strategies for utilizing technologies of production
- Strategies for utilizing technologies of sign systems
- Strategies for utilizing technologies of power
- Strategies for utilizing technologies of self

Worksheet for a Discourse Archaeology

Describe the problematic communication act to be assessed.

As you investigate the organization, use this chart to make notes of the role of technologies that contribute to the communication situation. Questions are provided for each area to begin your analyses. This section should lay the foundation for the structure of an analysis section.

A brief guide to Foucault's technologies[15]:
- Technologies of production: discourse strategies that create, transform, or manipulate the situation
- Technologies of sign systems: discourse strategies that construct meaning in the situation
- Technologies of power: discourse strategies that are imposed on individuals compelling them to behave a certain way
- Technologies of self: discourse strategies that are chosen by individuals to harness personal satisfaction

What technologies of production problematize the communicative act?

---

[15] Motion, J., & Leitch, S. (2009). *On Foucault*. In Ihlen, Ø., van Ruler, B., & Fredriksson, M. (2009). *Public Relations and Social Theory*. New York: Routledge.

What technologies of sign systems problematize the communicative act?

What technologies of power problematize the communicative act?

What technologies of self problematize the communicative act?

Working from the notes you made above, describe opportunities the organization has to transform the communicative act by making intentional changes in each set of technologies.

This section will form the foundation for the strategies section of the plan. Discuss the suggestions for each area separately in this section similar to the analysis. Whereas the analysis addressed the current state of discourse in the organization, the strategies should discuss the future/possible ways that the organization could address or transform the act. Try to develop multiple ideas in each area.

Strategies to employ technologies of production

Strategies to employ technologies of sign systems

Strategies to employ technologies of power

Strategies to employ technologies of self

John A. McArthur

Applying Giddens: Structural Analysis

A structural analysis, based in Giddens' Structuration Theory[16], examines the structures present in a scenario and the role of human agency in reproducing of transforming those structures. For scenarios related to change management or restructuring of a brand or organization, a structural analysis may prove effective at revealing unseen factors that impact the change.

In the analysis phase, the assessor defines the three types of structures present in the communication scenario:
- Structures of signification
- Structures of legitimation
- Structures of domination

Then, the assessor investigates agency by describing the current practices observed that reproduce or transform those three types of structures.

---

[16] For further information on Giddens' theory and its application for strategic communication, see Falkheimer, J. (2009). *On Giddens*. In Ihlen, Ø., van Ruler, B., & Fredriksson, M. (2009). *Public Relations and Social Theory*. New York: Routledge.

In the strategy phase, the assessor uses the organization's goals and mission to discern whether the structures need to be reproduced or transformed, and uses the following framework for offering suggested strategies for the scenario:
- Strategies to (reproduce or transform) structures of signification
- Strategies to (reproduce or transform) structures of legitimation
- Strategies to (reproduce or transform) structures of domination

Worksheet for a Structural Analysis

As you investigate the structures present in an organizational environment, use this chart to make notes about the properties of the structures you notice.
A brief guide to Giddens' structures[17]: • Structures of Signification: rules and resources that describe meaning in a situation • Structures of Legitimation: rules and resources established by norms, habits, and cultural factors. • Structures of Domination: rules and resources commanded through power and authority.
What structures of signification appear in the environment?

---

[17] Falkheimer, J. (2009). *On Giddens*. In Ihlen, Ø., van Ruler, B., & Fredriksson, M. (2009). *Public Relations and Social Theory*. New York: Routledge.

Structural Analysis

What structures of legitimation appear in the environment?

What structures of domination appear in the environment?

Of the three types of structures, what is the most commonly applied structure? How are the structures balanced?

Working from the notes you made above, choose one structure to focus upon. Describe the way that this structure is reproduced in the organization. opportunities the organization has to enhance its messaging by making intentional changes in each area.

For example, how is this structure taught to new members? What is the origin of the structure? Who has the power to change it?

This section will form the foundation for the analysis section of the plan. Repeat the above question for each identified structure.

Working from the notes you made above, describe any opportunities the organization has to act upon the structure. If the structure needs to be reproduced, how might that occur? If the structure needs to be transformed, how might that occur?

This section will form the foundation for the strategies section of the plan. Repeat the process above for each structure. Discuss the suggestions for each set of structures separately in this section similar to the analysis.

John A. McArthur

Applying Goffman: Impression Analysis

An impression analysis, grounded in Goffman's dramaturgic metaphor[18], can examine the messaging of an externally facing discourse. An impression analysis might be aptly applied to any external facing communication in which the audience needs to connect with the communicator – from public speaking to branding.

In the analysis phase, the assessor evaluates audience's perception of previous messaging attempts based on four key concepts from Goffman's drama metaphor:
- Impression management
- Framing
- Footing
- Face

---

[18] For further information on Goffman's theory and its application for strategic communication, see Johansson, C. (2009). *On Goffman*. In Ihlen, Ø., van Ruler, B., & Fredriksson, M. (2009). *Public Relations and Social Theory*. New York: Routledge.

In the strategy phase, the assessor uses the goals for the messaging scenario to discern possible actions and uses the following framework for offering suggested strategies for the scenario:
- Strategies to enhance messaging through impression management
- Strategies to enhance messaging through framing
- Strategies to enhance messaging through footing
- Strategies to enhance messaging through face

Worksheet for an Impression Analysis

As you investigate the organization, use this chart to make notes of the role of the communicators that contribute to the communication situation.

Questions are provided for each area to begin your analyses. These sections should lay the foundation for the structure of an analysis section. In the analysis take each of Goffman's ideas separately and for each of the four sections:

(1) describe the current state of the concept in the organization, and
(2) discuss how the concept is currently applied.

A brief guide to Goffman's concepts[19]:
- Impression management: information selected to appear on the frontstage vs. information retained backstage
- Framing: lenses through which information is presented
- Footing: the overlapping roles of the author, animator, and principal
- Face: the negotiation of positive and negative face between communicators

---

[19] Johansson, C. (2009). *On Goffman*. In Ihlen, Ø., van Ruler, B., & Fredriksson, M. (2009). *Public Relations and Social Theory*. New York: Routledge.

Impression Management

What communication is intended to be distributed (frontstage)? How successful is its messaging?

What communication is distributed that was unintended (backstage becoming frontstage?

What issues (if any) surround an incongruence between frontstage communication and organizational ideals (mission, vision, values, or backstage processes)?

Framing

What lenses or vantage points does the organization use to send the message?

Are these lenses the same as the ones used by message recipients?

Footing

Who is the principal of the message (where does the concept originate)?

Who is the author of the message (where is the content designed)?

Who is the animator of the message (who delivers the message and in what medium)?

Do all three parties concur on the message?

Face

How does the message contribute to the organization's prestige or image?

How does it attempt to "save face" from its audience by asserting goodwill?

How does it attempt to "threaten face" of its recipients by asserting power?

Working from the notes you made above, describe opportunities the organization has to enhance its messaging by making intentional changes in each area.

This section will form the foundation for the strategies section of the plan. Discuss the suggestions for each area separately in this section similar to the analysis. Whereas the analysis addressed the current state of impression management in the organization, the strategies should discuss the future/possible ways that the organization could address messaging. Try to develop multiple ideas in each area.

Opportunities to enhance Impression Management

Impression Analysis

Opportunities to enhance Framing

Opportunities to enhance Footing

Opportunities to enhance negotiation of Face

Applying Habermas: Discourse Analysis

A discourse analysis, based in Habermas' Theory of Communicative Action[20], examines the claims of discourse in a specific communication message. For scenarios related to an isolated communication message that went awry or a pervasive or systemic issue with audience knowledge or trust, a discourse analysis may prove beneficial.

In the analysis phase, the assessor evaluates audience's perception of the effectiveness of a communication message along four types of claims:
- Intelligibility
- Truth
- Truthfulness
- Legitimacy

---

[20] For further information on Habermas' theory and its application for strategic communication, see Burkhart, R. (2009). *On Habermas*. In Ihlen, Ø., van Ruler, B., & Fredriksson, M. (2009). *Public Relations and Social Theory*. New York: Routledge.

In the strategy phase, the assessor uses the goals for the communication message to discern possible actions and uses the following framework for offering suggested strategies for the scenario:
- Strategies for developing intelligibility
- Strategies for developing truth
- Strategies for developing truthfulness
- Strategies for developing legitimacy

Worksheet for a Discourse Analysis

As you investigate an isolated communication message or a systemic communication issue, use this chart to make notes about the properties of the message that contribute to misunderstanding.
These sections should lay the foundation for the structure of an analysis section. For each claim presented, evaluate the communication message as it exists currently.

A brief guide to Habermas' concepts[21]:
- Intelligibility: Both sender and receiver can physically understand and mutually agree upon the meaning of the message
- Truth: Both sender and receiver agree that possible truth exists in the message
- Truthfulness: Both sender and receiver demonstrate trust toward one another
- Legitimacy: Both sender and receiver accept the message as valid.

---

[21] Burkhart, R. (2009). *On Habermas*. In Ihlen, Ø., van Ruler, B., & Fredriksson, M. (2009). *Public Relations and Social Theory*. New York: Routledge.

Intelligibility

What did the sender intend the message to mean?

What did the receiver interpret the message as meaning?

What barriers or misunderstanding caused a lack of intelligibility (an incongruence between sender and receiver)? Often, these are physical barriers such as word choice, linguistic patterns, cultural differences, or misarticulation of phrases.

Truth

What components of the message do the sender and receiver agree are true?

What components of the message lack agreement?

Truthfulness

How does the sender demonstrate trust to the receiver? And, does the receiver notice this display of trust?

How does the receiver demonstrate trust to the sender? And, does the sender notice this display of trust?

Is deception a consideration for either the sender or the receiver? If so, how?

Legitimacy

Legitimacy cannot usually exist if all three of the preceding conditions are not met.

How does the sender articulate the validity (or lack of validity) of the message?

How does the receiver articulate the validity (or lack of validity) of the message?

If all three other conditions are met, why is the message not being accepted as valid?

Working from the notes you made above, describe opportunities the organization has to enhance its messaging by making intentional changes in each area.

This section will form the foundation for the strategies section of the plan. Discuss the suggestions for each area separately in this section similar to the analysis. Whereas the analysis addressed the current state of discourse in the organization, the strategies should discuss the future/possible ways that the organization could address messaging. Try to develop multiple ideas in each area.

Strategies to develop Intelligibility

Strategies to develop Truth

Strategies to develop Truthfulness

Strategies to develop Legitimacy

John A. McArthur

Applying Putnam:
Social Analysis

An internal social analysis, based in Putnam's concept of social capital[22], examines the creation of social coherence and its application in a community of members. For scenarios related to internal community building and development of organizational trust and internal reputation, Putnam can provide a window into the community or cultural sentiment of an organization.

In the analysis phase, the assessor identifies the two types of social capital:
- Bonding capital
- Bridging capital

Then, the assessor describes the realized impacts of identified capital on:
- Reputation
- Trust/Mis-trust

---

[22] For further information on Putnam's theory and its application for strategic communication, see Luoma-aho, V. (2009). *On Putnam*. In Ihlen, Ø., van Ruler, B., & Fredriksson, M. (2009). *Public Relations and Social Theory*. New York: Routledge.

In the strategy phase, the assessor uses the organization's goals and mission to develop opportunities to achieve those goals, using the following framework for offering suggested strategies for the scenario:
- Strategies for developing bonding capital
- Strategies for developing bridging capital
- Resulting strategies for impacting reputation
- Resulting strategies for impacting trust

Worksheet for a Social Analysis

As you investigate the internal community in an organization, use this chart to take notes about the role of social capital in the community. These sections should lay the foundation for the structure of an analysis section in the plan.

A brief guide to Putnam's concepts[23]:
- Bonding Capital: resources that act as glue that holds social groups together
- Bridging Capital: resources that develop relationships between social groups, connecting one group to resources outside of its own circle.
- Reputation: overall prestige of the social group resulting from the application of social capital
- Trust/Mistrust: perceived goodwill of the social group resulting from the application of social capital

---

[23] Luoma-aho, V. (2009). *On Putnam*. In Ihlen, Ø., van Ruler, B., & Fredriksson, M. (2009). *Public Relations and Social Theory*. New York: Routledge.

Social Analysis

Based on your observations, draw the organization being studied. Highlight, circle, or color code the people who make up social groups in the organization. What natural groups emerge? How (or through whom) are groups connected to other groups?

Draw another picture of the organization, this time starting with and spacing the groups, like a mind map. Then, connect them with lines to each other using the connections previously identified.

Social Analysis

Evaluate your drawing and answer the following questions.
These questions will form the framework of your analysis section.

How is bonding capital currently being applied in the organization?

How is bridging capital currently being applied in the organization?

What is the impact of these applications of social capital on reputation (for individuals in the organization and/or for the organization overall?

What is the impact of these applications of social capital on trust or mistrust (for individuals in the organization and/or for the organization overall?

Working from the notes you made above, describe opportunities the organization has to develop or address issues in social capital.
This section will form the foundation for the strategies section of the plan. Discuss the suggestions for each area separately in this section similar to the analysis. Whereas the analysis addressed the current state of social practice in the organization, the strategies should discuss the future/possible ways that the organization could use social capital. Try to develop multiple ideas in each area.

Strategies to develop bonding capital

Strategies to develop bridging capital

Strategies to develop reputation through the application of capital

Strategies to develop trust through the application of capital

John A. McArthur

Applying Weber: Legitimacy Claim Analysis

An analysis of legitimacy claims, based in Weber's concepts of legitimacy and legitimation[24], examines the means whereby an organization has established its credibility and can suggest a plan for credibility maintenance. For scenarios when an organization finds itself in defense of or needing to defend its processes or overall structure, an analysis of legitimacy claims can suggest an actionable path forward.

In the analysis phase, the assessor identifies the situation at hand and the need for legitimacy in the scenario. Then, the assessor breaks down the claims (assumptions/causal factors) present in the scenario and studies the ways that the organization has built each claim. Possible ways to build claims would include:
- Rational Grounds
- Traditional Grounds
- Charismatic Grounds

---

[24] For further information on Weber's theory and its application for strategic communication, see Wæraas, A. (2009). *On Weber*. In Ihlen, Ø., van Ruler, B., & Fredriksson, M. (2009). *Public Relations and Social Theory*. New York: Routledge.

In the strategy phase, the assessor uses the organization's goals and mission to explain the need for continued defense (or perhaps the lack of defensibility of an organization's claims, if necessary) and argues for ways to position those needs through the three paths to organizational legitimacy.

Worksheet for an Analysis of Legitimacy Claims

Jot down, based on observations and interviews, your understanding of the problem in the communication context.
Describe the issues surrounding credibility in the context of the problem. Free writing or mapping would be a helpful tool here.

Legitimacy Claim Analysis

Identify the causal elements that have led to a breakdown in credibility. major themes in your notes and list them here.

Choose one claim in your list above and describe how the organization has developed legitimacy around that claim. Specifically, you should address each grounding element of legitimacy for each claim. In your analysis section, repeat this process for each major claim you identified.

A brief guide to the three grounds[25]:
- Rational Grounds: a foundation in specified rules and the role of authority.
- Traditional Grounds: a foundation in the traditions, habits, or customs of the organization.
- Charismatic Grounds: a foundation on the interpersonal appeal of a single person with exceptional personal characteristics.

---

[25] Wæraas, A. (2009). *On Weber.* In Ihlen, Ø., van Ruler, B., & Fredriksson, M. (2009). *Public Relations and Social Theory.* New York: Routledge, p. 304.

How has the organization built a rational argument for this claim?

How has the organization built a traditional argument for this claim?

How has the organization built a charismatic argument for this claim?

Working with the claim identified above, determine if the claim is central to the organization's mission or otherwise problematic. If it is in agreement with the mission, then identify ways the organization can use the three grounds to support the claim. If the claim runs in opposition to the mission, discuss how the three grounds can be used to refute the claim.

In your strategy section, repeat this process for each identified claim.

Look back at the list of identified claims. What other questions do you need to ask the organization to tailor your suggestions to the organization's mission?

John A. McArthur

About the Author

Dr. John A. McArthur is associate professor of communication in the James L. Knight School of Communication at Queens University of Charlotte in North Carolina. His research focuses on the intersections of communication, information design, and proxemics. His focus on strategic communication practice originated in his work with students in the Knight School's Master of Arts in Communication program and the natural consultancies that exist in the banking town of Charlotte, NC, the 17th largest city in the United States.

Students in Dr. McArthur's courses have utilized the techniques in this worktext to improve communication practices in organizations of all sizes and address communication problems that run the spectrum of strategic communication practice. These strategies have been useful nationwide and across fields of influence from banking to creative and brand management to human resources.

Dr. McArthur has consulted with businesses, non-profits, technology start-ups, and universities and is available as a speaker and consultant for business, community, and academic audiences.

John A. McArthur
jamcarthur.com

Made in the USA
Middletown, DE
02 June 2015